# Amazing Animals
# Meerkats

Please visit our web site at www.garethstevens.com.
For a free catalog describing our list of high-quality books, call 1-800-542-2595 (USA) or 1-800-387-3178 (Canada).
Our fax: 1-877-542-2596

Library of Congress Cataloging-in-Publication Data

Ciovacco, Justine.
   Meerkats / by Justine Ciovacco.—U.S. ed.
      p. cm.—(Amazing Animals)
     Originally published: Pleasantville, NY: Reader's Digest Young Families, c2007.
     Includes bibliographical references and index.
     ISBN-10: 0-8368-9098-1   ISBN-13: 978-0-8368-9098-3 (lib. bdg.)
   1. Meerkat—Juvenile literature.  I. Title.
   QL737.C235C56 2009
   599.74'2—dc22                       2008013379

This edition first published in 2009 by
**Gareth Stevens Publishing**
A Weekly Reader® Company
1 Reader's Digest Road
Pleasantville, NY 10570-7000 USA

This edition copyright © 2009 by Gareth Stevens, Inc. Original edition copyright © 2006 by Reader's Digest Young Families, Pleasantville, NY 10570

Gareth Stevens Senior Managing Editor: Lisa M. Herrington
Gareth Stevens Creative Director: Lisa Donovan
Gareth Stevens Art Director: Ken Crossland
Gareth Stevens Associate Editor: Amanda Hudson

Consultant: Robert E. Budliger (Retired), NY State Department of Environmental Conservation

Photo Credits
Front cover: Dreamstime.com/Nico Smit, Title page: Dreamstime.com/James Hearn, Contents page: Roberta Stacy, pages 6-7: iStockphoto.com/Nico Smit, page 8: iStockphoto.com/Chris Fourie, page 9: iStockphoto.com/Neal McClimon, page 11: Dreamstime.com/Tina Rencelj, page 12: Roberta Stacy, pages 14-15: iStockphoto.com/Pavel Pospisil, page 16: iStockphoto.com/Robert Taylor, page 17: Steve Cukrov/Shutterstock Inc., page 17: Timothy Craig Lubcke/Shutterstock Inc., page 19: iStockphoto.com/John Neuner, page 20: Evon Lim Seo Ling/Shutterstock Inc., page 21: iStockphoto.com/rickt99, pages 22-23: iStockphoto.com/Nico Smit, page 24: Digital Vision, page 27: Roberta Stacy, page 28: Brian Wathen/Shutterstock Inc., page 31: iStockphoto.com/Iwona Dost Gorecka, pages 32-33: iStockphoto.com/Chris Fourie, page 34: Roberta Stacy, page 37: iStockphoto.com/Nico Smit, pages 38-39: Corbis Corporation, page 43: Adrian T Jones/Shutterstock Inc., pages 44-45: iStockphoto.com, page 46: iStockphoto.com/rickt99, Back cover: Stephen Coburn/Shutterstock Inc.

Every effort has been made to trace the copyright holders for the photos used in this book, and the publisher apologizes in advance for any unintentional omissions. We would be pleased to insert the appropriate acknowledgements in any subsequent edition of this publication.

Printed in the United States of America

1 2 3 4 5 6 7 8 9 10 09

# Amazing Animals
# Meerkats

By Justine Ciovacco

**Gareth Stevens**
Publishing

A WEEKLY READER COMPANY

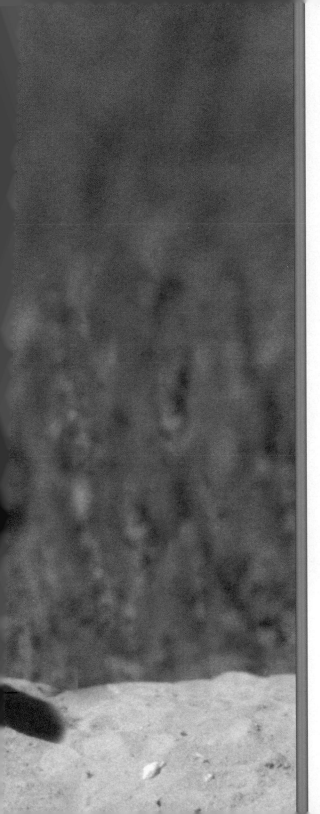

# Contents

# Chapter 1
# A Meerkat's Day

### Another Name

Some people call a meerkat a suricate (pronounced SUHR ih cate). That's because the meerkat's scientific name is *suricata suricatta*.

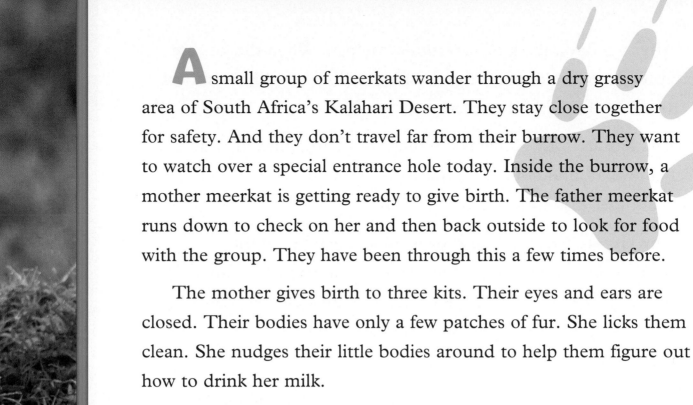

A small group of meerkats wander through a dry grassy area of South Africa's Kalahari Desert. They stay close together for safety. And they don't travel far from their burrow. They want to watch over a special entrance hole today. Inside the burrow, a mother meerkat is getting ready to give birth. The father meerkat runs down to check on her and then back outside to look for food with the group. They have been through this a few times before.

The mother gives birth to three kits. Their eyes and ears are closed. Their bodies have only a few patches of fur. She licks them clean. She nudges their little bodies around to help them figure out how to drink her milk.

## Wild Words

Meerkats live together in a group called a **mob** or a colony. The meerkats that have the most young are called the **alpha female** and the **alpha male**. All meerkat babies are called **kits**.

After ten days, the kits' ears and eyes open. When the kits are about four weeks old, they stop drinking milk. The adult members of the colony bring food to them.

The kits are fully grown when they are six months old. They freely move around outside the burrows, soak up the sun, and play. But they also must learn to find food.

The kits are taught to hunt by a female member of the group. But she is not their mother. Her special job is teaching. She teaches all the kits in the group how to hunt. She is great at tracking the scent of insects under the sand. And she's an expert at catching and cutting up a scorpion!

The kits watch their teacher as she runs her snout along the sand in search of insects. When she hears something moving below the surface, she digs down through the sand with her claws. She sees the insect, jabs at it, and gobbles it down.

The kits follow her lead and look for their own places to dig. The older meerkats will continue to bring them food until the youngsters are able to find food completely on their own.

**Family First**

A meerkat is ready to be a mother or father when it is a year old. But it may have to wait until its own mom and dad stop having youngsters. Until then, the young adults must help take care of their new brothers and sisters.

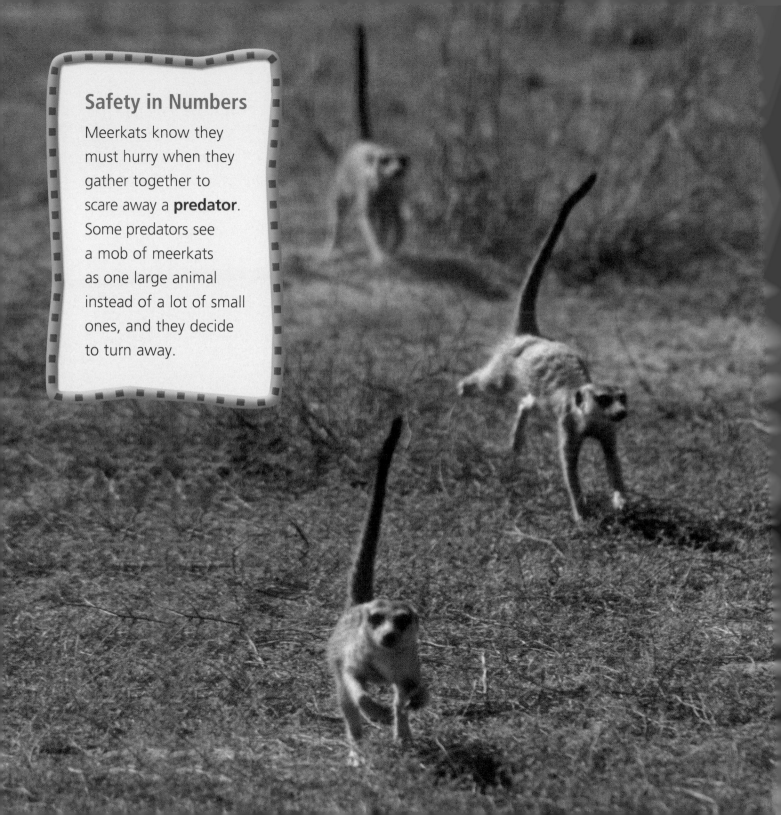

## Safety in Numbers

Meerkats know they
must hurry when they
gather together to
scare away a **predator**.
Some predators see
a mob of meerkats
as one large animal
instead of a lot of small
ones, and they decide
to turn away.

One morning, all the meerkats pop up out of their burrow as they always do. After lying in the sun for a while, they begin to look for food. One meerkat stands on guard and watches for predators. He sees an eagle flying above the colony's **territory**. He makes a high-pitched peeping sound to warn the group to get ready for a fight.

A few adults rush the kits back into the burrow. The remaining adults gather together. They dig quickly in the sand to create puffs of dust. This confuses the eagle. It makes the meerkats hard to see.

At the same time, the meerkats all stand up on their hind legs. They stretch their bodies tall and move close together. Growling and snarling, they jump up and down. They are trying to look like one giant, scary animal. And it works! The eagle turns and flies away.

## Wild Warrior

If a meerkat can't get to its burrow during an attack, it may lie down on its back. But it's not playing dead. It waves its claws around wildly and opens its mouth to show its teeth. This meerkat is showing the predator that it has many sharp tools ready!

Chapter 2
# The Meerkat's Body

A meerkat's tail is like a bike's kickstand. It helps the meerkat stand up straight on its hind legs without losing its balance.

# Body Basics

All meerkats have a coat that is a mix of gray, orange, and tan fur—except for the throat, which is a grayish white color. Dark-brown stripes run across their backs. Each meerkat has its own unique stripe pattern!

All meerkats have a tail with a black tip. The tail is usually the same color as the meerkat's stripes. The black tip is a big help to meerkats. They keep their tails up in the air when they look for food so they can easily spot one another.

Meerkats need to rest often because they use a lot of energy watching for danger and searching for food. This is one reason meerkats spend a lot of time basking in the sun.

## Hot Spot

A meerkat's belly has a small patch with almost no hair on it. A meerkat's dark skin shows through underneath. This patch helps a meerkat **regulate** its body temperature.

# Face Facts

A meerkat's face makes a real point! Its nose sticks out 2 to 3 inches (5 to 8 centimeters) from its face. Inside its snout are tiny, sharp teeth.

Meerkats spend a lot of time in the sand, digging. The meerkat's eyelid has a special membrane. It acts like a windshield wiper by removing sand from the eye. Meerkats can see faraway things very well and at angles around them.

The tiny ears of meerkats stick out from the sides of their heads. Amazingly, the ears don't fill up with dirt while the meerkats dig. Meerkats can close their ears to make the openings very small.

## Surely Sharp

The meerkat's four sharp canine teeth are typical of animals that eat only meat. Canine teeth hold onto **prey** so it can't run away.

The dark circles around a meerkat's eyes make the eyes appear larger to some animals. This may even help scare them away! The circles also absorb some of the sun's rays, which lets meerkats look directly at the sun while watching out for eagles.

Meerkats are very fast diggers. They can dig out as much dirt as their own body weight in a couple of seconds!

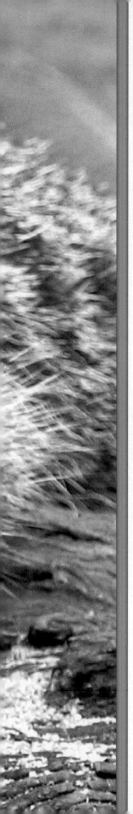

# Dig Those Claws

Meerkats use all four paws when they dig, which helps them to dig very quickly. Each paw has four sharp claws. The claws stick out all the time and are curved. They are great for digging.

Meerkats also use their sharp claws to kill prey. Sometimes they will then drag the prey, such as a millipede, across the sand with the tips of their claws. To meerkats and some other animals, millipedes have an awful smell and taste. Dragging a millipede through the sand seems to help "clean" it and make it more appealing to eat.

Meerkats are excellent climbers. They climb easily, like cats. Their claws are a big help, as are their strong back legs.

## Tippy Toes

A meerkat looks tall when it stands on its back legs. The paws on the back legs are long. Meerkats do not stand on the soles of their feet, as people do. They stand on their toes.

# Chapter 3
# The Mob Rules

Babysitters may go without food for as long as a day while they watch over the colony's newborns.

# All for One

Meerkats live in groups of three to five families. These groups, which may total up to 40 members, are called mobs or colonies. Each meerkat in a mob usually has its own job, but it will also share jobs with other meerkats. All the members help each other when looking for food, teaching and protecting their young, and defending against predators.

All meerkat jobs are very special. Here's what they do:

• Hunters look for food. All meerkats do this for themselves most of the time, but hunters help find food for the kits. They will also find food for the babysitters.

• Babysitters stay near the den with the kits and protect them while the other meerkats are hunting. Female babysitters provide milk for the young, just like their moms.

• Teachers show young meerkats how to hunt for food.

• Guards, also known as sentinels, watch the land and sky for predators. They usually stand on their hind legs on top of a high spot, such as a log or a mound of sand. They sound out warning signals if they see, hear, or smell a predator.

# A Is for Alpha

Meerkat mobs do not have one leader. But there is an alpha male and an alpha female that usually have all or almost all of the babies. They can sometimes act as the leaders because their jobs are so important. If other meerkats have babies, they can be kicked out of the mob by the alphas.

Most alpha females give birth about once a year. One female can have as many as thirty-two kits in her lifetime. Alphas need a lot of help with all of the kits they have!

A meerkat usually stays with the family it was born into and with the colony in which it grew up. If the colony gets too large, an adult meerkat who is ready to mate may move into another colony.

### Move On!

When a meerkat colony has eaten all the available food in one area, they move on and dig new burrows in another area. Most colonies move four or five times a year.

Staying close together and grooming each other helps the members of a meerkat mob to work as a group.

Meerkats usually hide and run from each other before settling down to play-fighting.

# Fighting for Their Rights

Meerkats enjoy wrestling and fighting with each other. It's a way for them to show their feelings. Young kits will wrestle over food that adults have brought to them. Adults don't mind this kind of play-fighting. It helps the young ones practice defending themselves against predators.

Females also make fighting moves, such as jumping and snapping, to let males know they are ready to mate.

# Cool and Careful

Meerkats are smart and learn fast. They are one of the few animals that are "taught" how to hunt for food by adults.

Meerkats are said to have short memories. Why? Because they have been known to kill any meerkat that has been away from the colony for more than six hours! The meerkats in the colony are often just being extra careful, in case the meerkat turns out to be an attacker. If the meerkats can stay calm and take the time to smell the new arrival, they can figure out that they already know him.

# Home Sweet Home

Meerkat mobs live in underground homes called burrows. The burrows, which are dug by the meerkats, are made up of long tunnels that connect rooms. The average meerkat burrow is about 10 feet (3 meters) long and has about 15 rooms. Each burrow can have up to 70 entrances so the meerkats can run inside to hide!

Inside the burrow, a meerkat mob is protected from hot days and cold nights. On cold nights, the members of the colony huddle together to stay warm.

Meerkats mark the entrances to their burrow with saliva and urine to warn other animals away. They move into a new burrow about every other month, depending on the supply of food. They will stay in the burrow where their young were born for about three weeks. They will not move until the kits are strong enough.

Sometimes meerkats will share their home with ground squirrels and yellow mongooses. These three types of animals don't eat the same foods, so they can share a territory. But meerkats keep their newborns safe by keeping them away from the visitors.

Meerkats leave their burrow entrances one at a time. This way, the first one out can look for danger.

# Chapter 4
# The Meerkat Menu

Meerkats spend up to four or five hours a day searching for food. While digging in the sand for a meal, they sometimes dig themselves into a hole!

# Fast Food

Meerkats are **carnivores** (pronounced CAR nih vorz). They only eat meat. They can grab small, fast-moving food such as worms, beetles, and other insects. They are also able to catch and eat small **mammals**, lizards, and some snakes.

Meerkats are one of the few animals in the world that kill and eat scorpions. Scorpions have deadly poison on their stingers, but adult meerkats are able to bite off the stingers and survive.

It takes a lot of practice for meerkat kits to learn to kill scorpions. At first, adult meerkats catch and kill the tasty meal for the kits. They bite off the **poisonous** stingers before giving them to the little ones. Then the lessons get tougher. The adults bite the stingers off live scorpions, but the kits must kill the now harmless creatures by themselves. The adults will bring a scorpion back if it runs away from the kit. After a lot of practice, meerkat kits are able to hunt and kill scorpions by the time they are four months old.

# On the Lookout

Meerkats find a lot of their food by looking and listening downward. Keeping their heads down makes them easy targets for predators, such as jackals, hyenas, snakes, eagles, and even other meerkat mobs that move into their territory.

Some meerkats stand guard while the other meerkats hunt for food. The guards make a low, steady peeping sound when all is well. They will change to a fast, high-pitched peeping sound as a warning if one of them sees a predator.

The meerkat's excellent vision lets it spot an animal very far away—farther than three football fields!

Meerkats act fast when a predator is near. First, they try to dive underground or under any bushes. If there is nowhere to hide, they will come together and fluff out their fur. They will jump up and down and hiss and snarl. Babysitters don't join in these group scare demonstrations. Their job is to find a place to hide the kits.

## Human Interest

Meerkats quickly learn which animals are dangerous. Over time, meerkats learn to ignore people watching and photographing them. They will even move closer to see what the humans are doing.

A guard, or sentinel, will stand in place and watch for enemies for an hour or two at a time. Then a new guard will take over.

# Chapter 5

# Meerkats in the World

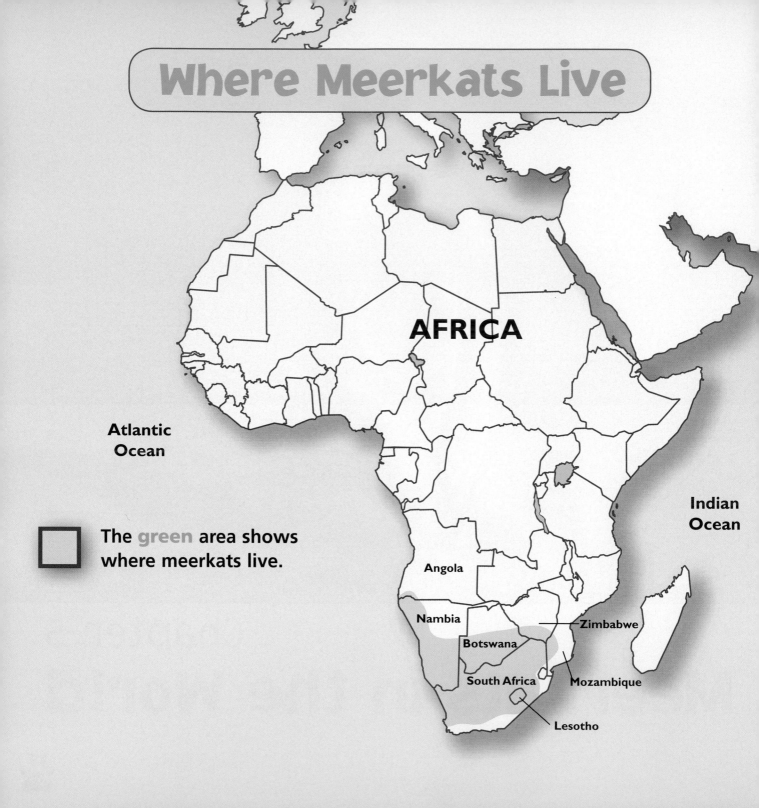

# Where Meerkats Live

AFRICA

Atlantic
Ocean

The green area shows
where meerkats live.

Indian
Ocean

Angola

Nambia

Botswana

Zimbabwe

South Africa

Mozambique

Lesotho

# Home Sweet Home

Meerkats live in and around the Kalahari Desert in southern Africa. Their homes can be found in the countries of Angola, Namibia, Botswana, Zimbabwe, Mozambique, Lesotho, and South Africa.

Meerkat country is hot and dry. There are times when it doesn't rain for many months. These periods are called droughts. During a long drought, desert plants can die. The insects and other animals that depend on plants for food can die, too. The meerkats then need to move farther away to find food. If all of the mob members are hungry and looking for food, then there are fewer members able to act as guards. This leaves the weakest meerkats as easy prey for attackers.

### Africa's Angels

In some parts of Africa, the meerkat is known as the sun angel because it loves the sun so much!

# The Future of Meerkats

Meerkats exist in large numbers. However, the life of a meerkat is not an easy one. Natural threats are droughts, burrow-flooding rainstorms, and attacks by predators. Kits are the most affected by these events. Only one kit in four survives its first year.

Smaller mobs have more trouble surviving than larger mobs. Fewer meerkats means less help with kits and fewer guards to take turns watching for predators. Colonies of 15 to 30 seem to have the best chance of survival.

## Fast Facts About Meerkats

| | |
|---|---|
| **Scientific name** | *Suricata suricatta* |
| Class | Mammalia |
| **Order** | Carnivora |
| Size | Up to 20 inches (51 cm) from head to tip of tail |
| **Weight** | Up to 2 pounds (1 kg) |
| Life span | Up to 14 years |
| **Habitat** | Burrows in dry, desertlike lands |

**Meerkats have learned that they need to stay together to survive.**

# Glossary

**alpha female** — lead female of the mob. She is usually the only one to give birth.

**alpha male** — lead male of a mob. He is usually the only one to mate with the alpha female.

**balance** — the ability to stay steady

**carnivore** — a meat-eating animal

**habitat** — the natural environment where an animal or plant lives

**kit** — a baby meerkat

**mammal** — an animal with a back-bone and hair on its body that drinks milk from its mother when it is born

mob — a group of meerkats. This
group is also called a colony.

poisonous — containing a harmful
or deadly poison

predators — animals that hunt and
eat other animals to survive

prey — animals that are hunted by
other animals for food

regulate — to control

species — a group of plants or
animals that are the same in
many ways

territory — an area of land that an
animal considers to be its own
and will fight to defend

# Meerkats:
# Show What You Know

How much have you learned about meerkats? Grab a piece of paper and a pencil and write your answers down.

1. What are meerkat babies called?

2. Why do meerkats keep their tails in the air when they are looking for food?

3. How do meerkats keep their ears from filling up with dirt when they dig?

4. Why do meerkats have a dark patch of skin on their stomachs?

5. What is a group of meerkats called?

6. Why do meerkats leave their burrows one at a time?

7. Why is it possible for meerkats to share their territory with ground squirrels and yellow mongooses?

8. How many rooms does the average meerkat burrow have?

9. What poisonous creature are meerkats famous for eating?

10. On what continent do meerkats live?

1. Kits 2. So they can easily spot each other 3. They close their ears 4. To help regulate their body temperature 5. A mob or a colony 6. So that the first one can look out for danger 7. Because they don't eat the same foods 8. 15 9. Scorpions 10. Africa

# For More Information

## Books

*Meerkat Manor: Flower of the Kalahari*. Clutton-Brock, Tim (Touchstone, 2008)

*Meerkats*. Early Bird Nature Books (series). Storad, Conrad J. (Lerner Publications, 2006)

*Mob of Meerkats*. Animal Groups (series). Moore, Heidi (Heinemann, 2004)

## Web Sites

### Mammals: Meerkat

*http://www.sandiegozoo.org/animalbytes/t-meerkat.html*

Besides reading about meerkats and their lives together, check out Photo Bytes, which features images of these animals, and listen to a meerkat's bark.

### Meerkat

*http://animals.nationalgeographic.com/animals/mammals/meerkat.html*

Find meerkat fast facts, a map and globe showing the range of meerkats in Africa, an engaging video, and more.

**Publisher's note to educators and parents**: Our editors have carefully reviewed these Web sites to ensure that they are suitable for children. Many Web sites change frequently, however, and we cannot guarantee that a site's future contents will continue to meet our high standards of quality and educational value. Be advised that children should be closely supervised whenever they access the Internet.

# Index